CW01498769

HENRY E. MEJIA

EXCEL CHARTS and GRAPHS NINJA

HENRY E. MEJIA

EXCEL CHARTS AND GRAPHS NINJA

Copyright © 2020 HENRY E. MEJIA

DEDICATION

To my parents, who have taught me that life is about overcoming obstacles and enjoying it.

ACKNOWLEDGMENTS

I would like to thank all those who supported me throughout the creation of this book, either with words of encouragement or ideas for this book.

INTRODUCTION

Welcome to a new EXCEL NINJA book! The fastest, the most practice-based and definitely the most straightforward Excel Book Series you will ever find!

You will learn to use with confidence the most important and useful Excel CHARTS.

Excel Ninja Series is all about this:

- **Learning fast**
- **Having fun while learning**

- Learning trough practice (from the very beginning)
- No unnecessary fillers to make the book look longer
- The most straightforward and lean approach
- Getting results!

Loaded with a gigantic amount of practice spreadsheets, examples, and recommendations.

My goal for this Excel Ninja Series was to achieve the perfect balance between a lot of exercises and examples without compromising the straightforward approach, and that's what you will find here!

That being said, I would like to summarize the benefits of becoming an Excel CHARTS and GRAPHS Ninja:

- Increased chances of getting a promotion and better jobs (Because you are more productive and have better skills)
- Less workload (Excel does the heavy lifting)
- More free time
- Less stress
- A sense of growth (When you learn something new you feel great, and you know it!)
- Etc., etc.

I could spend more time, word and pages explaining to you the benefits and the importance of becoming an EXCEL CHARTS and GRAPHS NINJA, but I promised that I won't fill this book with unnecessary words so let's start the first chapter right now!

GET YOUR 26 PRACTICE SPREADSHEETS (.XLSX)

Before starting Chapter 1 I recommend you to get your 26 practice spreadsheets. Those exercise files are included for everyone who purchases this book. They will serve you at the end of each chapter to reinforce what you have learned and make sure you have learned it well.

All you have to do is to send me an email to:

ems.online.empire@gmail.com

With the Subject *"CHARTS AND GRAPHS NINJA PRACTICE SPREADSHEETS"* and saying:

"Hello, I bought your book EXCEL CHARTS AND GRAPHS NINJA and I

need the 26 practice spreadsheets"

I will gladly reply your email and send you the files.

Now you are ready to start Chapter 1. Let's go!

CHAPTER 1:

BOOK LAYOUT

In this brief chapter I want to explain to you the book layout. I really believe that it is a lot easier to navigate through this book if you know the exact order from the very beginning. Also, if you feel comfortable, you can skip certain parts and revisit them later, according to what you need at this moment.

First, in Chapter 2, I'm going to explain what a Chart is and exactly what it is for. Some people think that charts are used to embellish the work you have done but that is not exactly true. So, in Chapter 2 we are going to go deeply into this concept.

Next, in Chapter 3, I want to show to you

the most important types of Charts and to provide a fast but clear explanation of each one of them. You'll understand that each type of Chart serves to its own purposes. You will also learn that to believe that any Chart could do the work is a costly and common mistake among Excel user.

In the following Chapters (from Chapter 4 and beyond) we will go deep into each type of Chart individually. You will learn in which scenarios you need to use that specific type of Chart and in which scenarios you need to avoid it. You'll also learn the strengths and weaknesses of each Chart and the most important features you need to take care off when creating one. Also, as the most important part of each chapter, you will learn through practice by developing your own charts following the exercises provided in this book.

The last Chapter of this book gives you some extra advice on how you can become an Excel Ninja by developing your skills in other key Excel features.

That said, let's move on to the next chapter!

QUICK CHAPTER SUMMARY

- There are plenty types of Charts
- Each of them has its own and strengths and weaknesses
- The purpose of this book is to train you to use the chart type that you need in each situation you face.

CHAPTER 2:

WHAT IS A CHART AND WHICH IS ITS TRUE OBJECTIVE?

In just a few words, a Chart is a visual representation of data. The data I'm talking about may be just a few values or a lot of them.

The main fact here is that a Chart transforms raw data into visual images that include proportions, time, variables, and some other features.

Charts transform data into images

What is even more important is the objective of those charts. Always remember that the reason you are creating a chart is to

TELL A STORY! That's it.

The only reason to create and show a chart is to communicate the story the data is hiding. You see, when you have lots of disorganized (or even organized) numbers, it is so hard to tell if things are going the way you want or not. Even if you are a numbers maniac (like me) sometimes you may find it hard to recognize the patterns inside those numbers.

But, when you organize those numbers and create a visual representation of them, you can easily communicate that story to everyone you need.

If you need to show the story of previous years' profits, you need a chart that allows you to show quantity and time relationship.

If you need to tell a story about the sales made by each division of the company, you need a chart that allows you to show proportion (not time).

If you need to show the strengths of your employees, based on specific features, you need a chart that allows you to show all the features at the same time.

I think I have made my point so far. You will need to use the specific chart type that allows you to tell the story you want to tell in the best way possible!

So, remember:

The only reason to create a chart is to tell a story

QUICK CHAPTER SUMMARY:

- Charts transform data in to visual representations
- Charts tell stories
- Specific chart types tell specific stories

CHAPTER 3:

TYPES OF CHARTS (GENERAL EXPLANATION)

Here is one of the most important chapters of the book, because we are going to discover the chart types and you will get a general understanding on how they are commonly used.

The main purpose of this chapter is to serve as a brief introduction to the specialized chapters, where we will focus on each of the charts individually.

Please notice that when talking about charts, there are some important thing that we want to convey to our audience. Those things fall in one or more of these categories:

- Development over time
- Proportion of a whole
- Relationship between variables
- Distribution of data

BAR CHART

The Bar Chart is probably the most used kind of chart and it is super useful. It consists on multiple vertical bars with different height, according to the variable that you are measuring.

However, it has its limitations and it should not be used when facing certain situations.

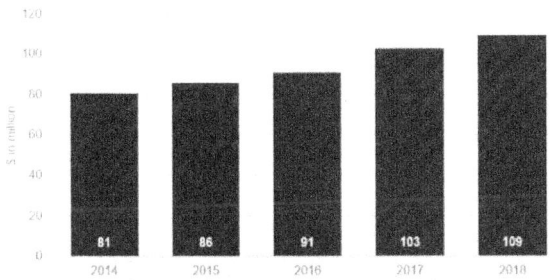

The bar chart is excellent to show the

development of one variable over time and it also could be used to show the relationship between more variables at a specific point in time.

You can't add too much information to this chart because it would be a mess. With Bar charts, the less information, the better.

PIE CHART

Pie charts are absolutely the best way to show all the parts of a whole. It is like a Pie with colored slices inside it and it is the one to use when you need to convey proportions.

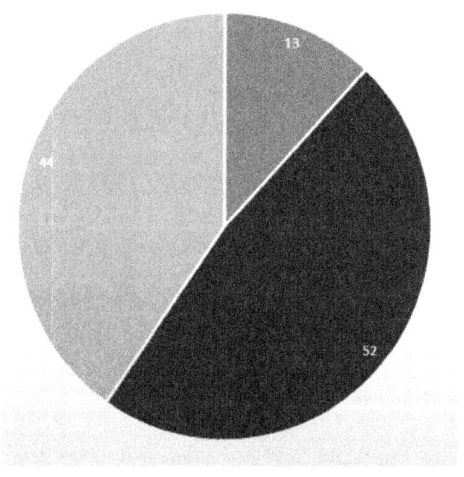

The only important requirement here is that you must include all the parts of the whole (100%). If you miss one slice, you would be giving incorrect information to you audience.

LINE CHART

Line charts are formed with lines moving from the left to the right. The benefits of them using continuous lines is that they make it easy to follow a trend, thus, line charts are best used to follow the development of multiple variables over time (something that the bar chart can not do).

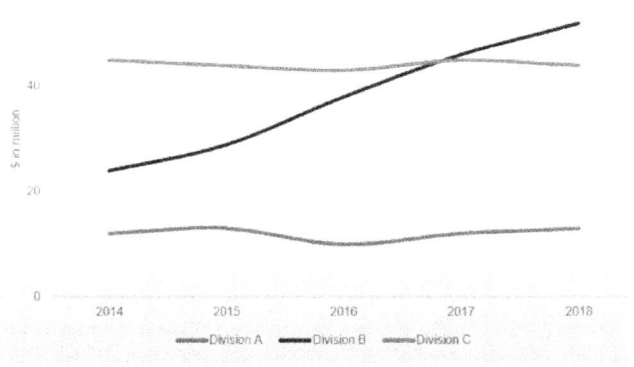

Unlike bar charts, with line charts you

can't show the relationship of 1 variable at a specific point in time, but you do can track the development of multiple variables over time.

AREA CHART

Area chart is similar to the line charts (they are kind of brothers) but they are best used for different purposes.

While line charts are used to track the development of multiple variables over time, area charts are best used to convey the proportion in which every variable contributed to the complete output over time.

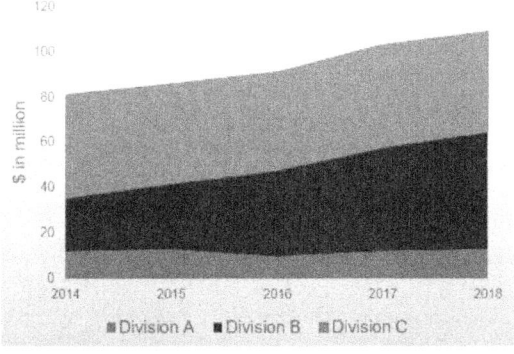

There are two different area charts that

you will learn to use. Stacked Area Chart and 100% Stacked Area Chart.

TREEMAP CHART

Treemap charts or "Rectangular Charts" are the way to go if you have to show subdivisions of the parts of a whole. What??? Let me explain it better.

Do you remember the Pie chart? It showed the parts of a whole (proportions). With Treemap charts you can show the subdivisions of each part, and at the same time show the parts of the whole.

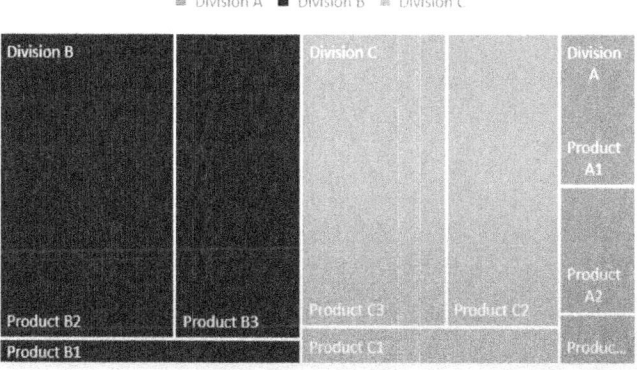

This chart is used to show Proportions

only! You mustn't mess with development over time here. Treemaps are used only to show proportions at a specific point in time.

BRIDGE CHART

Bridge charts are interesting because they show the process the variable went through. They can also convey how the parts of a whole contributed to the current result.

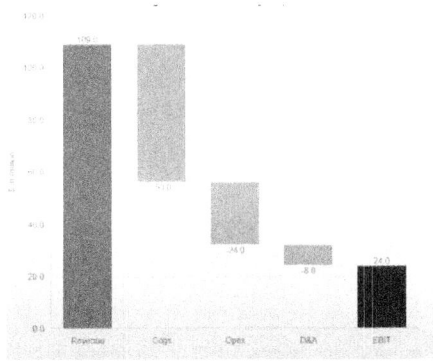

So, the emphasis on a bridge chart is not the start or the end, but the process and how the variable got there.

SCATTERPLOT CHART

This kind of chart is mostly used in the field of statistics. Whenever you want to watch the distribution of data, this is the chart to go.

Obviously, there is no time involved here. There is just collected data that is shown as a little dot in the chart.

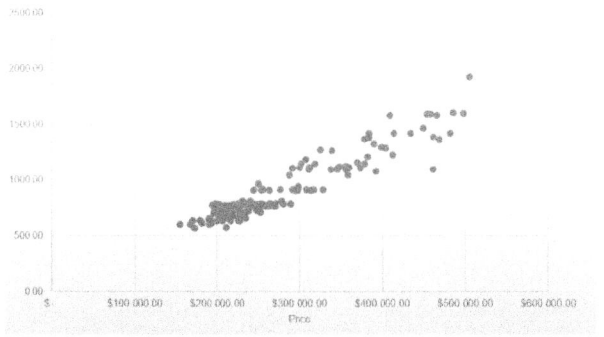

The main use of this chart is to identify is you have found a pattern or if you have just random data.

HISTOGRAM CHART

The last kind of chart that you are going to learn is the Histogram chart. This is also used in statistics and also used to show distribution.

The main difference between the previous type is that Histogram charts show Distribution and Quantity.

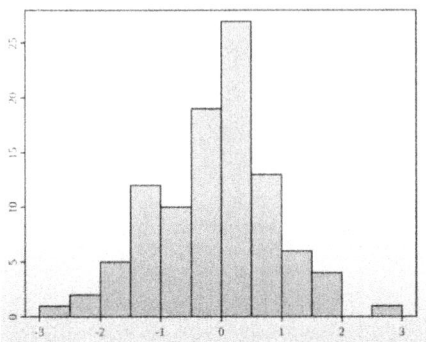

You get to see the quantity of data that you have in each of the ranges.

QUICK CHAPTER SUMMARY:

- You have the option to use several types of charts that are used for different situations
- Each type of chart has its own strengths and weaknesses

- Also, each kind of chart has its own restrictions

CHAPTER 4

CHART TYPE #1
BAR CHART (COLUMN CHART)

Bar Charts are the first type that you need to master. We all remember our years at school and probably this was one of the first charts that we watched.

Just for you to know, Bar Charts and Column Charts are almost the same. Excel names "Bar" charts the ones that create HORIZONTAL bars, and "Column" charts the ones that create VERTICAL columns.

Column charts are mostly used and they are commonly called "Bar" charts by almost everybody. So, in this chapter I'm going to call them "Bar" charts, just please have in mind that both Horizontal and Vertical work the same.

So, as I told you previously, Bar Charts are one of the easiest ways to convey simple things visually. While the Y axis (vertical) shows the amount or quantity of the variable, the X axis could show the development trough time or different variables at the same time.

SITUATIONS TO USE BAR CHARTS:

- **You face a situation with 1 or 2 variables, at most.**

- o **Something and Time:** For example, you need to convey Sales development over Time (Sales and Time), or Spending over Time (Spending and Time).

- o **Something vs Something:** For example, you need to communicate the Earnings of each Store you own in the city (Earnings vs Earnings vs Earnings). Although you may have 10 stores, the variable remains the same, Sales.

- **You face a situation with less than 10 inputs:** By Inputs I mean entries.

  - o Taking the previous example, if you owned 50 stores instead of 10, the bar chart would be a mess and you wouldn't be able to communicate anything because it would be visually cluttered. Perhaps you could categorize your 50 stores in 4 or

5 regions and then show that as a bar chart.

SITUATIONS TO AVOID BAR CHARTS:

- **You face a situation when you need to convey proportions.** Trying to show the proportion that 1 store contributes to Overall Earnings is impossible with Bar Charts.

- **You face a situation when you need to convey proportions AND development over time.** Obviously, this is even more impossible with Bar Charts.

- **You face a situation when you need to convey distribution.** Although Bar Charts may seem like Histogram Charts, showing distribution is kind of different because you need to convey "Ranges" and "Repetition of Choice", thus, Histogram Charts are used frequently when surveying. Please do not mixed both of them in your brain, you'll understand it better in the Histogram Chart chapter.

- **You face a situation when you need to show the middle steps it took to get to the end result.** With Bar Charts you just get the end result, not the way you got there.

SHOW TIME! (Open file Chapter4ex1.xlsx)

Now let's solve the first exercise! "But, how am I going to solve something if I have not learned it yet??" you may ask, but my teaching style is through practice from the very beginning, so you'll learn by doing it and by making mistakes, that's the best way for you to learn!

SITUATION:

Some superheroes had to join together to start a grocery store business because the economic crisis left them unemployed! Each of them had to take care of one location (store). Now, at the annual meeting, their accountant needs to SHOW them the revenue each one of their stores made.

By the way, you are their accountant! So, let's get started and build the chart. Here is the data.

SUPERHERO	REVENUE	
Optimus Prime	$	141,248
Naruto Uzumaki	$	186,401
Batgirl	$	133,560
Green Lantern	$	444,027
Krillin	$	305,249
Aragorn	$	103,101
Zorro	$	239,929
Black Panther	$	223,380
Catwoman	$	472,094

Doctor Strange $ 361,080

STEP 0: You have to know that it doesn't matter if the data table is Vertical (like the one above) or Horizontal (like the one below).

SUPERHERO	Optimus Prime	Naruto Uzumaki
REVENUE	$ 140,804	$ 346,643

(Partial table)

With the bar chart you get to choose if the bars show up Vertical or Horizontal, being Vertical the most common for both the table and the chart.

STEP 1: Ask yourself What do I need to convey? **In this situation, you need to show a general view of revenue per store.** So a simple Bar Chart would do it.

STEP 2: Select the table completely, from A2 to B12 (From "Superhero" to "157,646"

STEP 3: Go to "Insert" tab, select the Bar Chart icon

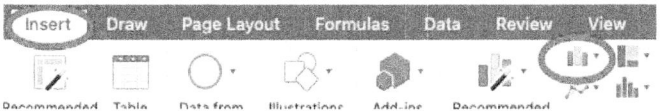

Then, you basically have 3 main options (Pick the first one, Clustered Column)

- Clustered Column
- Stacked Column
- 100% Stacked Column

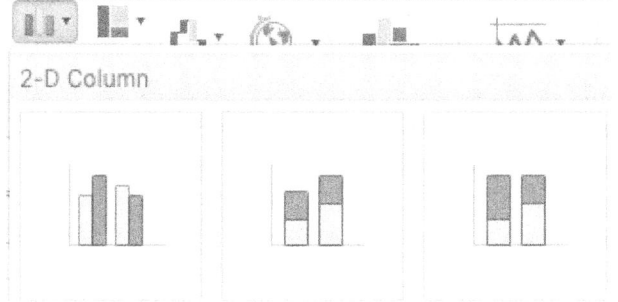

You are going to learn the 3 of them, although the most used is the Clustered Column

NOTE: You have also the following options with their own variants:

- 3D Columns: They work the same as 2D Columns
- 2D Bars: They work the same as 3D Columns, the only difference is that the Bars appear Horizontally. Thus, this Chart is a better option when you have lots of data inputs.
- 3D Bars: They are the same as 2D Bars.

STEP 4: You'll get the chart instantly. And you can easily SEE (Visualize) who did better and who did worse.

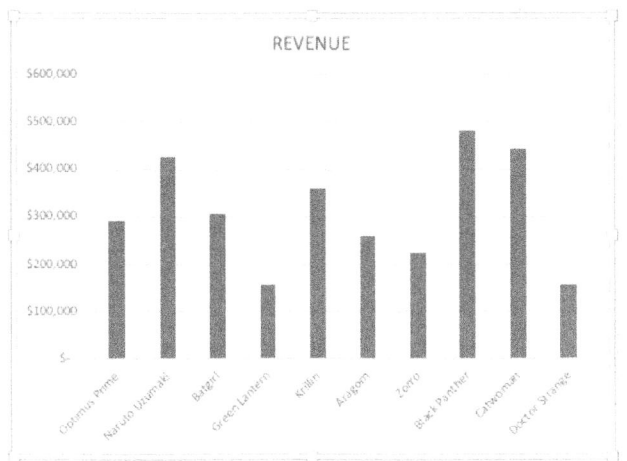

WHAT HAPPENS IF YOU WANT TO CUSTOMIZE YOUR CHART AND MAKE IT PRETTIER?

STEP 1: Click inside the chart, then click Chart Design, and pick one of the different templates that you have there.

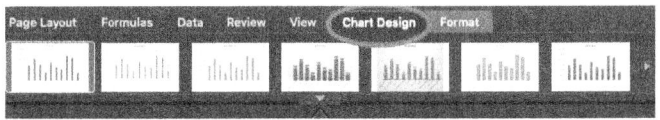

Some of them add the number label on top of the column, some of them change the background color, etc.

STEP 2: Left Click on any bar, select Format Data Series and then change the color of the bars by selecting the Color Buckets

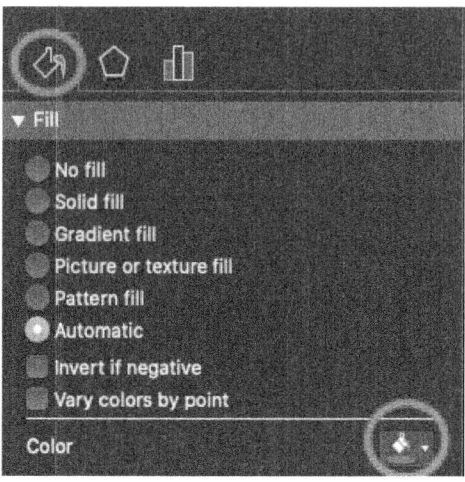

Congratulations! You have created your first Chart!

The following exercise is going to help you understand the difference between 2 variables Column Chart, Stacked and 100% Stacked Bar Charts.

SHOW TIME! (Open file Chapter4ex2.xlsx)

Now let's solve a similar exercise. The main difference is that you have the Revenue of 2 years, and you need to create a simple Bar (2D Column) Chart with this.

SUPERHERO	2019	2020
Optimus Prime	$ 291,597	$ 225,187
Naruto Uzumaki	$ 427,460	$ 194,288
Batgirl	$ 307,652	$ 164,432
Green Lantern	$ 158,784	$ 333,568
Krillin	$ 360,637	$ 403,510
Aragorn	$ 258,470	$ 588,275
Zorro	$ 223,530	$ 423,274
Black Panther	$	$

	482,393	224,833
Catwoman	$ 444,633	$ 236,664
Doctor Strange	$ 157,646	$ 433,021

STEP 1: Ask yourself What do I need to convey? **You need to show the growth or decrease in the revenue between 2019 and 2020.** So, you need a Bar Chart inserting the 2 years (2 variables)

STEP 2: Select the whole table (A2:C12)

STEP 3: On your Ribbon select INSERT, go to the chart section and within 2-D Column section select the first one, **Clustered Column**.

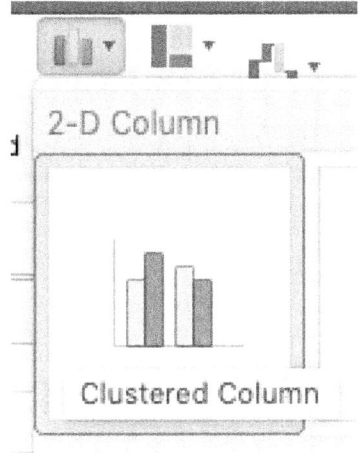

You'll get something like this.

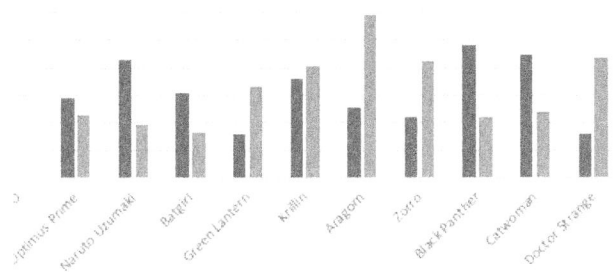

This chart shows which stores grew their revenue and which decreased their Revenue, comparing 2019 and 2020. You can easily see thar Aragorn was the one that increased the revenue the most and holds the #1 position in 2020. Black Panther was the best in 2019 but the revenue decreased significantly in 2020 in his store.

But what if your main focus is to convey the overall revenue (2019 and 2020 combined) of each store?...

SHOW TIME! (Open file Chapter4ex3.xlsx)

STEP 1: Ask yourself What do I need to convey? **You need to show the overall revenue (2019 and 2020 combined).** So, you need a Stacked Column Chart that <u>shows both years in 1 single column!</u>

STEP 2: Select the whole table (A2:C12)

STEP 3: On your Ribbon select INSERT, go to the chart section and within 2-D Column section select the second one, **Stacked Column**.

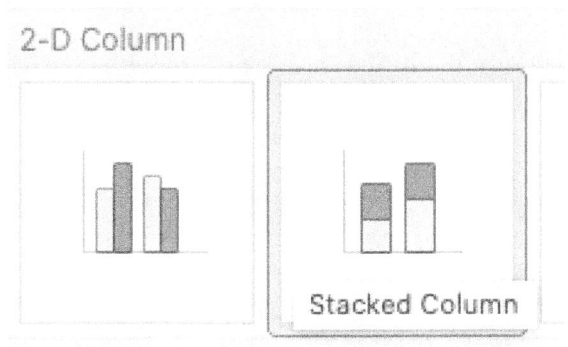

You'll get something like this.

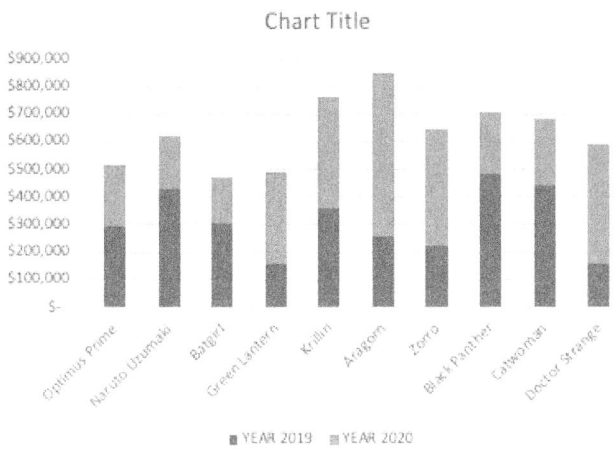

(You can double click the title to change it)

Look how this chart tells the same history but in a different way, and with a different focus. Note that Krillin didn't grabbed our attention in the Clustered

Column chart, but with the Stacked Column chart Krillin did grab our attention by being the 2nd best manager overall.

Did you see how creating another type of Column Chart or Bar Chart helps you to convey different things?

Now, what about the 100% Stacked Column Chart? How does it work?

Open file Chapter4ex4.xlsx

You will find that, similarly to the Stacked Chart, the 100% Stacked Column chart combines the 2 years in each bar. However, the Columns in the 100% Stacked chart are all of the same height, thus representing the 100% of each Manager (Hero).

Overall, the 100% Charts (Line and Columns) show the contribution (in percentage) of each variable to the final result. In other words (and within the context of this exercise), the contribution of each year to the final result in each store.

STEP 1: Ask yourself What do I need to convey? **You need to show the overall revenue (2019 and 2020 combined) AND to show the proportion (percentage) each year contributed to the OVERALL RESULT OF EACH STORE.** So, you need a 100% Stacked Column Chart that <u>shows both years in 1 single column!</u>

STEP 2: Select the whole table (A2:C12)

STEP 3: On your Ribbon select INSERT, go to the chart section and within 2-D Column section select the second one, **100% Stacked Column Chart.**

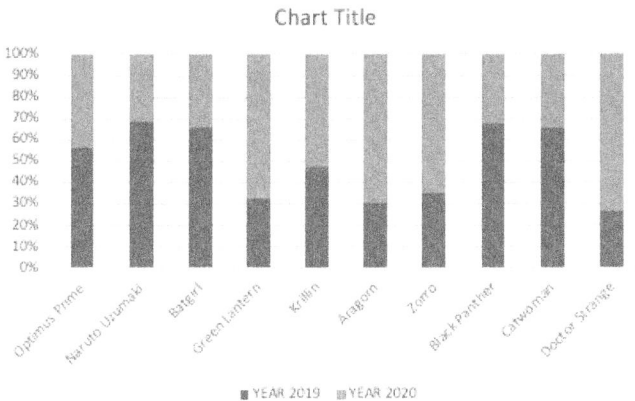

Now you can arrive at some good insight:

Notice how Naruto, Batgirl, Black Panther and Catwoman are losing sales compared to the previous year. Also notice hoy Green Lantern, Aragorn and Dr. Strange increased their sales tremendously, they must be doing something well.

For this reason (and with the help of a 100% Stacked Chart), if were the financial advisor to all of them, I would ask Green Lanters, Aragorn and Dr. Strange what they are doing and truly ensure that everybody else does the same thing.

CONGRATULATIONS!! You have finished the Bar/Column Chart Chapter!!

MORE EXERCISES:

- Chapter4ex5.xlsx
- Chapter4ex6.xlsx
- Chapter4ex7.xlsx

QUICK CHAPTER SUMMARY:

- Bar Charts and Column Charts are almost the same, although Column Charts (vertical columns) are more used than Bar Charts (horizontal columns).

- To create Bar and Column Charts the process in excel is the same.

- Regular Column or Bar Charts create one column/bar for each of the variables.

- Stacked Charts combine 2 or more variables in the same Column/Bar

- 100% Stacked Charts combine 2 or more variables of equal height, showing the proportion that each variable has impacted in the final result.

Are you enjoying this book?

Do you think it's easy to understand?

Have the exercises helped you learn faster?

Without knowing your opinion, I won't know if the book has helped you to become a better Excel user.

You can share your thoughts with me by writing a Review

CHAPTER 5

CHART TYPE #2
PIE CHART

Pie Charts are easily explained because they have that shape (the shape of a pie with slices). They are commonly used to convey the proportion of a whole.

Instead of saying "X department account for X percentage of the total spending in our company" and showing a list of numbers, why not just show the image itself? It is easier to communicate with images.

SITUATIONS TO USE PIE CHARTS:

- **You face a situation with just 1 variable, at this point in time.**

- o **Spending:** For example, you need to convey Spending among departments, or among companies within a conglomerate.
- o **Revenue:** Same situation as spending. It could also include Sales made by each Sales Representative
- o **Market Share:** To communicate which companies dominate X amount of the market.

SITUATIONS TO AVOID PIE CHARTS:

- **You face a situation when you need to convey proportions AND development over time.** This is not possible for pie charts.
- **You face a situation with more than 10 variables.** Although this is possible, it would look too cluttered.

- **You face a situation when you need to convey distribution.** Pie charts are not suitable for this
- **You face a situation when you need to show the middle steps it took to get to the end result.** Pie charts just show the end result.

SHOW TIME! (Open file Chapter5ex1.xlsx)

SITUATION:

Superman is running a big company, and needs to know the total spending of each department. Here is the data:

DEPARTMENT	REVENUE
SALES	$ 5,183,450
HUMAN RESOURCES	$ 1,140,163
FINANCE	$ 7,157,069
OPERATIONS	$ 4,151,574

R&D	$	7,455,601
PRODUCTION	$	2,430,892

STEP 1: Ask yourself What do I need to convey? **In this situation, you need to show how each department contributes to Total Spending.** So, a simple Pie Chart Would do it.

STEP 2: Select the table completely, from A2 to B12 (From "Department" to "2,430,892"

STEP 3: Go to "Insert" tab, select the Pie Chart icon and please, for this exercise, just select the 2-D Pie Chart.

Although I must say to you that you'll have 3 options in the first row:

- Pie
- Pie of Pie
- Bar of Pie (this one is the same as the Pie of Pie, but with a bar

instead, so I won't explain this one)

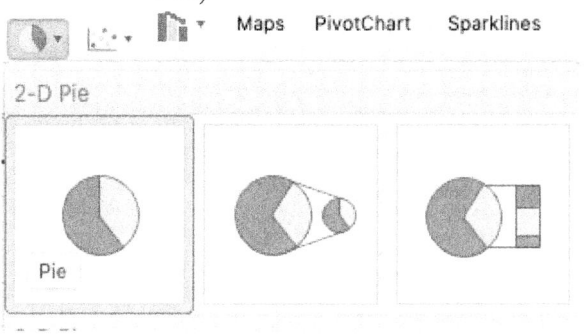

And below, you will also have the option of Doughnut chart.

But please, for this exercise, just select the 2-D Pie Chart (the simple and easy one)

STEP 4: You'll get the chart instantly. And you can easily see the proportion. But please, click on the chart, go to CHART DESIGN above in the ribbon, and SELECT STYLE 3. That Style shows the percentages also.

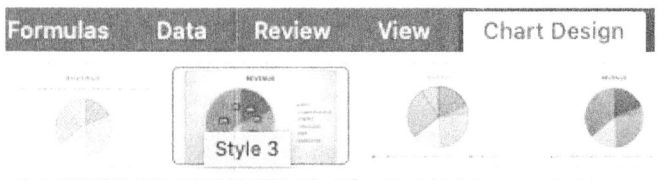

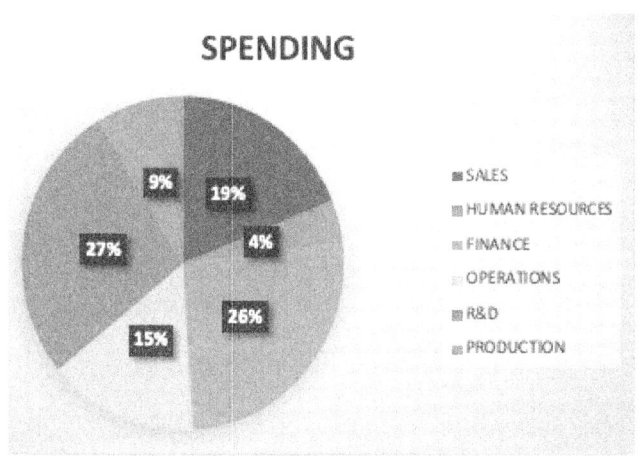

The reason why I like this Style 3 is because you get to see the actual percentages on each category. Therefore, is a great way to convey the story. You'll notice that R&D spending is the largest and Human Resources doesn't need that much money to run smoothly.

NOTE: Doughnut charts are just the same. The only difference is that you can manually insert the TOTAL AMOUNT in the middle of the doughnut to emphasize that amount. Because of this, whenever the Total Amount is more important that the pieces, you have better use a doughnut chart. If the pieces and percentages are more important that the total amount, you may use a Pie Chart

That said, let's continue with the next Exercise! Pie of the Pie!

SHOW TIME! (Open file Chapter5ex2.xlsx)

SITUATION:

Superman is running the same company, but the data shows a slightly variation. As you may see, I have introduced, R&D 1 and 2. So, Research and Development Department is divided in 2 parts. In this exercise, I would like to see the total spending by department AND the 2 parts of R&D.

DEPARTMENT	SPENDING
SALES	$ 5,183,450
HUMAN RESOURCES	$ 1,140,163
FINANCE	$ 7,157,069
OPERATIONS	$ 4,151,574
R&D 1	$ 3,213,847
R&D 2	$ 2,381,736

If you want a visual representation of this kind of data, you will need a PIE OF THE

PIE Chart

STEP 1: Ask yourself What do I need to convey? **In this situation, you need to show how each department contributes to Total Spending, AND you also need to separate R&D 1 and 2 and show them individually.** So, a simple Pie of Pie Chart would do it.

STEP 2: Select the table completely, from A2 to B12

STEP 3: Go to "Insert" tab, select the Pie of Pie Chart icon

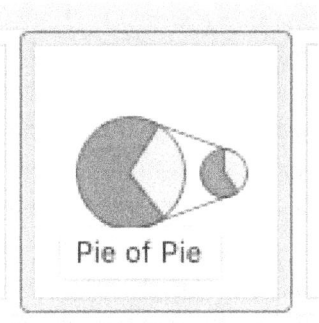

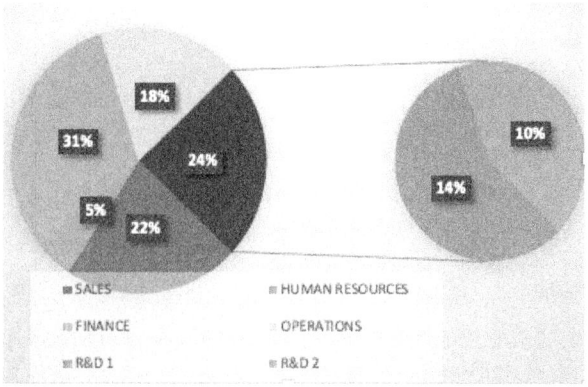

If you select the "Style 3" design for your chart, you will easily see that Research and Development has 24% of the total spending. Furthermore, R&D 1 contributes with 14% and R&D 2 contributes with 10%.

NOTICE: Automatically, the Pie of Pie chart creates the 24% area (Overall R&D) and then it splits them up in in the second Pie Chart.

Let's solve another exercise.

Open file Chapter5ex3.xlsx

Same thing as the previous exercise, the only difference is that now you have R&D 1,

2 and 3 AND you will use the BAR OF PIE Chart. Let's do it.

DEPARTMENT	SPENDING
SALES	$ 5,183,450
HUMAN RESOURCES	$ 1,140,163
FINANCE	$ 7,157,069
OPERATIONS	$ 4,151,574
R&D 1	$ 3,213,847
R&D 2	$ 2,381,736
R&D 3	$ 5,827,267

STEP 1: Ask yourself What do I need to convey?

STEP 2: Select the table completely, from A2 to B12

STEP 3: Go to "Insert" tab, select the Bar of Pie Chart icon

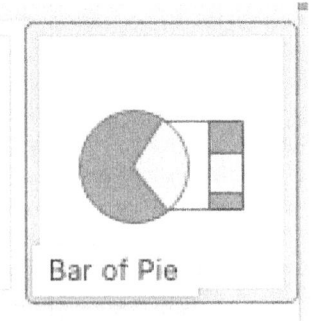

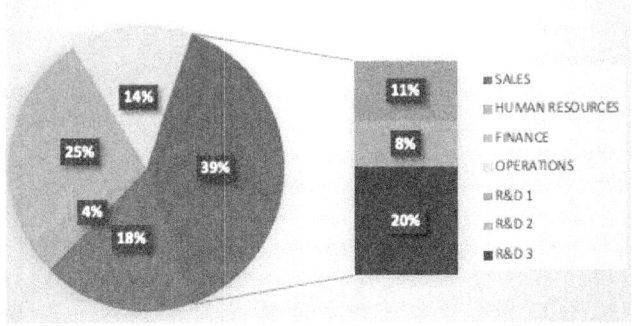

Notice how automatically the Chart identifies that R&D 1, 2 and 3 are subcategories.

But what happens if Excel doesn't identify the subcategories?

Step 1: Double click on the BAR (The one showing R&D 1, 2 and 3). To the left you are going to see a new set of controls.

Step 2: Go to "Values in second plot" and write 2, just to see what happens to the chart.

Notice how the Chart changes and just shows 2 items in the Bar (R&D 2 and 3).

If you change the "Values in second plot" to 4, you will notice that the Bar includes Operations and R&D 1, 2 and 3.

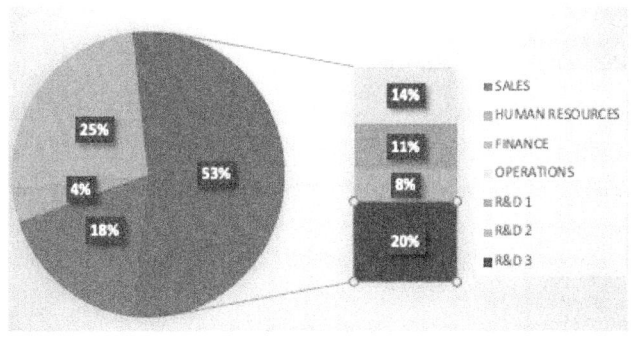

In simple words, "Values in second plot" tells excel hoy many items you want in the Bar, thus, excel removes them from the

Pie to insert them in the Bar.

CONGRATULATIONS! Now you have mastered Pie Charts!

MORE EXERCISES:

- Chapter5ex4.xlsx
- Chapter4ex5.xlsx

QUICK CHAPTER SUMMARY:

- Pie Charts are great when you need to convey the proportions of a whole.
- Pie Charts can't communicate development over time
- Pie Chart can show extra information by using Pie of Pie Charts
- Bar of Pie Charts also show extra information
- You can set the number of "subcategories" that a Bar of Pie shows, and you can do the same with Pie of Pie charts.

CHAPTER 6

CHART TYPE #3
LINE CHART

Line Charts are beautiful because they are easy to read and to understand. They are just lines plotted inside the chart, running from left to right. Therefore, Line charts are great to convey development over time of several variables.

Despite this, Line Charts have its own tricky feature: The Stacked Line Charts and the 100% Stacked Line Chart are awful! This is due to the Stacked feature itself. You see, to Stack up some lines creates confusion for the eye, and communicates nothing.

How can we solve this? With Area Charts (Explained in the next Chapter).

Consequently, in this chapter we are just going to learn regular Line Charts (Because Stacked Line charts suck!)

SITUATIONS TO USE LINE CHARTS:

- **You face a situation with several variables, AND want to show DEVELOPMENT OVER TIME.**
  - o **Spending over time:** For example, you need to convey Spending among departments over time.
  - o **Revenue over time:** Same situation as spending.
  - o **Population over time**
  - o **Pandemic cases over time**
  - o **Stock Price over time**
  - o You get the idea…

NOTICE: Because Line Charts are used to convey **DEVELOPMENT OVER TIME**, the X axis will almost always be a time measure (years, months, days, hours)

SITUATIONS TO AVOID LINE CHARTS:

- **You face a situation when you need to convey proportion.** This is not possible for line charts.
- **You face a situation with more than 10 variables.** Although this is possible, it would look too cluttered.
- **You face a situation when you need to convey distribution.** Line charts are not suitable for this
- **You face a situation when you need to show the middle steps it took to get to the end result.** Line charts just show the end result.

SHOW TIME! (Open file Chapter6ex1.xlsx)

SITUATION:

Four teams have been accepting hero

jobs since 2010, and their salaries have been increasing at different rates over time. The data includes 10 years, here is some part of the data

TEAMS	2010	2011	2012	2013
Z WARRIORS	$ 142,914	$ 154,347	$ 166,695	$ 180,030
AVENGERS	$ 214,763	$ 223,354	$ 232,288	$ 241,579
JUSTICE LEAGUE	$ 125,132	$ 141,399	$ 159,781	$ 180,553
NINJA TURTLES	$ 345,241	$ 352,146	$ 359,189	$ 366,373

Your job is to create a visual representation of their salaries and arrive at some conclusions.

STEP 1: Ask yourself What do I need to convey? **You need to convey the development over time of the salaries**

STEP 2: Select the table **but NOT completely**, just select from A3 to L6 (From Z Warriors to the last salary of 2020). Why? Because if you select the whole table, "TEAMS" would appear as another line.

STEP 3: Go to "Insert" tab, select the Line Chart icon

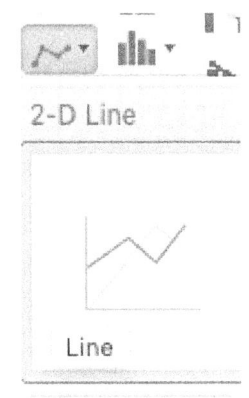

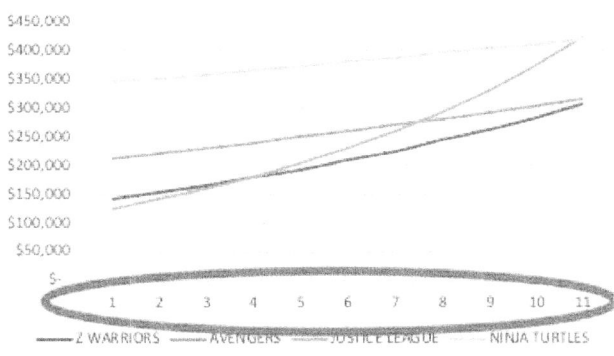

Notice that there is something incorrect there. The X Axis doesn't show the years. What we want is the chart to show "2010, 2011, 2012, etc.", so you are going to need 2 additional steps.

STEP 4: Left click the chart, the go to Chart Design Tab above in the Ribbon, and then click on "SELECT DATA"

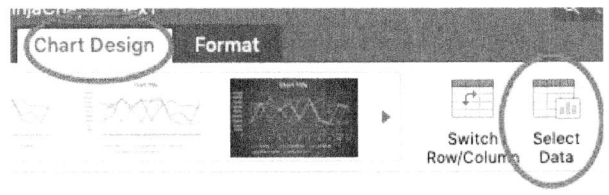

STEP 5: Find "Horizontal Axis Labels", click the little icon to the right, and select from 2010 to 2020 in the spreadsheet, the press Enter and click OK

That way, you will get the years in the X axis of the chart

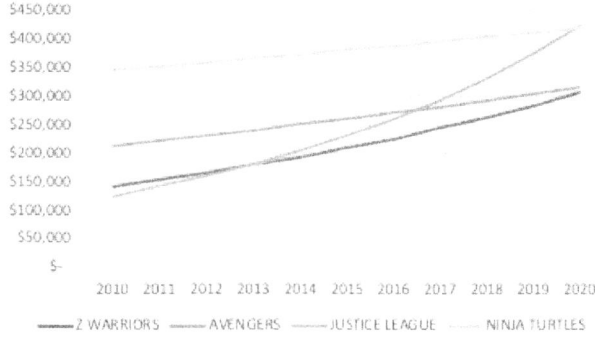

As you may see, Ninja Turtles started with a great salary, but the salary of Justice League members grew faster that every other team. Only Line charts can give you this kind of insights because they are so clean, they are not cluttered at all.

CONGRATULATIONS! You now know how to use Line Charts. As I told you before, Stacked Line Charts are not efficient so we are going to move to the Area Charts.

MORE EXERCISES:

- Chapter6ex2.xlsx

QUICK CHAPTER SUMMARY:

- Line Charts are excellent to convey development over time
- Stacked Line charts are not as great as you may think, because you get confused when you see them
- If you are going to use Line Charts, make sure you use Regular Line Charts
- If you want to use Stacked and 100% Stacked, you better use Area Charts

CHAPTER 7

CHART TYPE #4
AREA CHARTS

Area Charts are a great way to convey a complex story in a single image. In my opinion, Area Charts show detailed information to arrive at important conclusions, yet, they are not used as regularly as Bar, Line or Pie Charts.

Think of an Area Chart as a Line Chart with the background filled with colors. This single feature makes it easier for the eye to find details that otherwise would had been missed.

Unfortunately, regular Area Charts could be misguiding, because of the "filled background" (you will understand that in the first exercise), so the best way to use them is with Stacked and 100% Stacked Area Charts.

SITUATIONS TO USE STACKED AREA CHARTS:

- **You face a situation with several variables, want to show development over time AND WANT TO CONVEY HOW EACH VARIABLE CONTRIBUTES TO THE OVERA RESULT AND ALSO CONVEY THE OVERALL RESULT AT THE SAME TIME**
  - o **Overall Spending over time:** For example, you need to convey Spending among departments over time.
  - o **Overall Revenue over time:** Same situation as spending.
  - o **Population over time divided by country or regions.**
  - o **Overall diseases and the amount of each disease.**

o Overall profits and from where they are being made.

o Overall pieces of real estate and their locations by region or city.

o You get the idea…

NOTICE: Because Area Charts are used to convey **DEVELOPMENT OVER TIME**, the X axis will almost always be a time measure (years, months, days, hours)

SITUATIONS TO AVOID STACKED AREA CHARTS:

- **You face a situation with more than 10 variables.** It would be a mess.

- **You face a situation when you need to convey distribution at a specific time.** Area Charts are used for development over time

SHOW TIME! (Open file Chapter7ex1.xlsx)

SITUATION:

Let's solve the same Line Chart exercise from the previous chapter, just so you can visualize how a Regular Area Chart is not a good idea.

Four teams have been accepting hero jobs since 2010, and their salaries have been increasing at different rates over time. The data includes 10 years, here is some part of the data

TEAMS	2010	2011	2012	2013
Z WARRIOR S	$ 142,9 14	$ 154,3 47	$ 166,6 95	$ 180,0 30
AVENGER S	$ 214,7 63	$ 223,3 54	$ 232,2 88	$ 241,5 79
JUSTICE	$	$	$	$

LEAGUE	125,132	141,399	159,781	180,553
	$	$	$	$
NINJA	345,241	352,146	359,189	366,373
TURTLES				

Your job is to create a visual representation of their salaries and arrive at some conclusions using Area Charts.

STEPS: Follow the same Steps of the previous Chapter, just beware that in the 3rd Step you need to choose Line Charts and then 2D Area Chart.

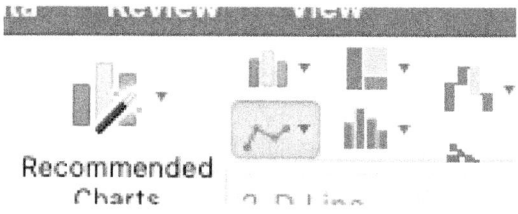

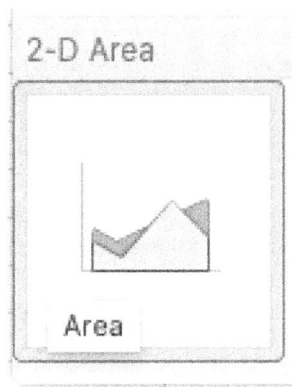

You will get this awful chart!

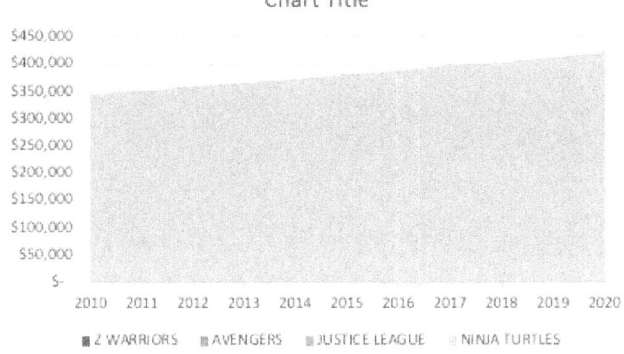

Why? Remember that Area Charts have their background filled with solid colors, so, that Chart shows the development of Ninja Turtles' salaries, but all the other salaries are BEHIND Ninja Turtles, and because Area charts have solid color backgrounds, YOU CAN NOT SEE THE OTHER

VARIABLES! That is why Regular Area Charts are not useful.

Let's solve the same exercise with a Stacked Area Chart.

Open file Chapter7ex2.xlsx

Follow the exact same process as the previous exercise, but instead of selecting 2d Area Chart, select Stacked Area Chart

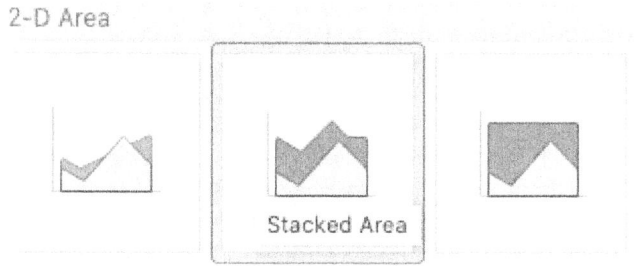

Then remember to change the name of the X axis by clicking on Select Data. You will get a beautiful chart like this one

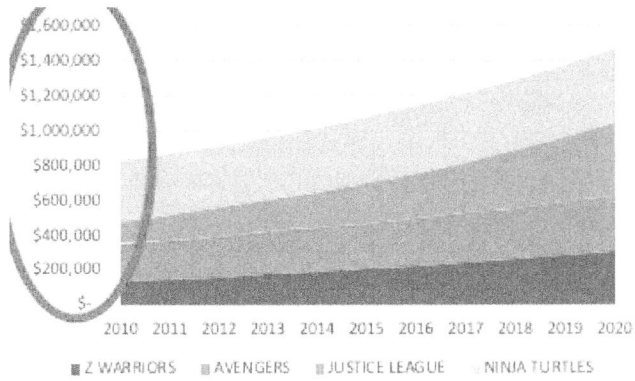

You have to notice several things:

- You are getting the overall amount in the Y axis. In other words, this Stacked Area Chart is adding every single salary at a given time (2010 as an example)

- As you move to the right, you are still getting the overall amount at each specific year.

- Also, you can easily see the distribution of that overall amount. You must observe that in 2010 Justice League represented just a little amount of the overall amount. Nevertheless, in 2020 Justice

League plays a very important role, getting almost the same salaries as Ninja Turtles.

- Finally, notice that the overall payroll has increased substantially over the past 10 years.

This is the power of a Stacked Area Chart: You can track the development over time of the OVERALL AMOUNT, as well as the development over time of each of the parts.

Now, let's look at the difference with a 100% Stacked Area Chart.

Open file Chapter7ex2.xlsx

Follow the exact same process as the previous exercise, but instead of selecting 2d Area Chart, select 100% Stacked Area Chart

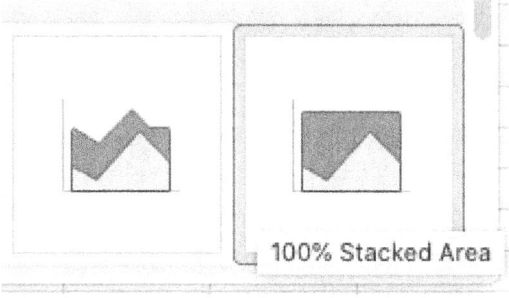

You'll get a chart like this one

With 100% Stacked Area Charts you have several things to notice:

- The Y axis shows a percentage that is always 100% for the Overall amount. In other words, you CAN NOT track the development over time of the Overall Amount, because it will always be 100%.

- What you do can track is the development over time of each of the variables AS A PERCENTAGE OF THE OVERALL AMOUNT.

- That said, 100% Stacked Area Charts are best used to track the development of each individual variable as a part of the overall.

- In the chart you may notice that Z Warriors and Avengers contributed with almost the same percentage, in other words, If the overall amount grew 10%, they also grew 10% more or less. Otherwise, Justice League increased their contribution to the overall result, and Ninja turtles decreased their contribution. We are not saying that Ninja turtles didn't grew, we are saying that they contributed with LESS PERCENTAGE.

MORE EXERCISES:

- Chapter7ex4.xlsx

QUICK CHAPTER SUMMARY:

- Area Charts are great to convey development over time and the contribution of each variable to the overall result
- Regular Area Charts are useless
- Stacked Area Charts convey the development over time of the OVERALL amount as well as the development of each variable.
- 100% Stacked Area charts DO NOT show the development of the overall result, but they do emphasize the development of each variable as a percentage of the overall result.

CHAPTER 8

CHART TYPE #5
TREE MAP CHARTS

Tree Map Charts are a great way to show the parts of a whole. Think of it as a Pie Chart on Steroids!

Tree Map Charts splits the whole thing in parts, and then splits the parts in smaller pieces! That way you can get the Big Picture of whatever you are studying.

It is also important to notice that Tree Map Charts are able to give information on a given specific time, so development over time is no suitable for this kind of charts.

SITUATIONS TO USE TREE MAP

CHARTS:

- You face a situation where you need to look at each part of the whole thing, and algo the subcategories:
  - The sales revenue of each sales executive of each product
  - The main products of each one of the divisions of a company.
  - The main expenditures of each one of the divisions of a company.
  - You get the idea…

SITUATIONS TO AVOID TREE MAP CHARTS:

- **You need to show development over time.** You simply can't do it.
- **You face a situation when you need to convey distribution at a specific time.** Area Charts are used to show proportion, not distribution, which is different.

SHOW TIME! (Open file Chapter8ex1.xlsx)

SITUATION:

You are the leader of the East division, you have 4 products and 3 salespeople for each product, and you need to discover which one is your best-selling product and whether all the salespeople is contributing to the overall result or not.

PRODUCTS	SALES EXECUTIVE	SALES
PRODUCT 1	Harry Potter	$ 454,737
PRODUCT 1	Captain America	$ 293,531
PRODUCT 1	Robin	$ 63,153
PRODUCT 2	Captain Marvel	$ 348,914
PRODUCT 2	Picollo	$ 455,249
PRODUCT 2	Batman	$ 161,870
PRODUCT 3	The Rocketeer	$ 401,637
PRODUCT 3	Superman	$ 153,589

PRODUCT 3	Batwoman	$	476,044
PRODUCT 4	Hawkeye	$	260,565
PRODUCT 4	The Incredibles	$	51,808
PRODUCT 4	Goku	$	203,511

STEPS: Repeat the steps of the previous exercise, and in Step 3 please choose Tree Map Chart

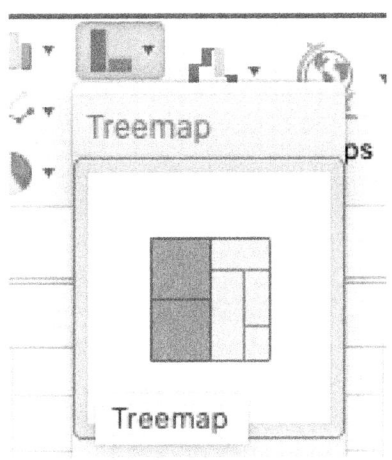

You'll get a nice chart like this one!

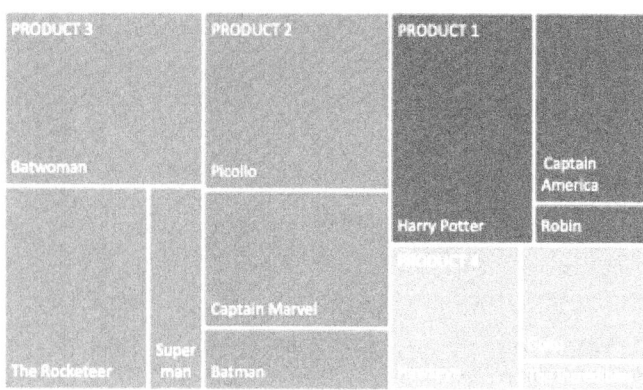

There are several things to notice with this chart:

- The whole rectangle represents the total amount of sales made by the sales team.

- It is so easy to discover that Product 4 is the least popular product and Products 1 and 2 are the best performers.

- Also, it is a piece of cake to discover the sales executives that aren't doing well. Superman and Batman are doing awful, even though they are selling the best-selling products. While Harry Potter and Hawkeye are doing great with products that are less popular.

CONGRATULATIONS! This is how you use a Tree Map Chart to get intel from the data you have.

MORE EXERCISES:

- Chapter8ex2.xlsx

QUICK CHAPTER SUMMARY:

- Tree Map Charts show the divisions and subdivisions of a whole
- This kind of chart is not suitable to convey development over time

Is an easy way to get insights about the big picture

CHAPTER 9

CHART TYPE #6
BRIDGE (WATERFALL) CHARTS

I believe we have covered in great detail 5 of the most useful types of charts: Bar (Columns), Pie, Line, Area and Tree Map. Nevertheless, we still have types more to learn, and in this chapter, it is the time for Bridge Charts.

Waterfall Charts are also called Bridge Charts, and they are great when trying to communicate the middle steps that took place in order to get to the final result. In other words, **Bridge Charts emphasize the middle steps**, not the final result.

Because of their nature (communicating steps) you could use them to show development over time or at a specific time.

As an example, if you want to show how the equity of a company grew over the previous 5 years emphasizing the 5 years (development over time) then you can use a bridge chart.

Also, if you want to show how different kinds of expenses reduced the profits at the close of the year (specific time) you can use a bridge chart.

SITUATIONS TO USE WATERFALL CHARTS:

- You face a situation where you need to emphasize the middle steps that led to a result:
  - Expenses that decreased profits
  - Months that had greater impact in your business
  - Etc
- You face a situation where you need to show the increases and decreases of a single variable

SITUATIONS TO AVOID WATERFALL CHARTS CHARTS:

- **You need to convey proportion of a whole.** You simply can't do it.
- **You need to compare the total value of several variables.** Not suitable for this task.

SHOW TIME! (Open file Chapter9ex1.xlsx)

SITUATION:

You are now in the financial department of a big company, closing the year. Your task today is to find out why the revenue (that was huge) turned out into a minor profit and SHOW that to your directors.

Revenue	$	545,039,182
Cost of production	-$	218,015,673
Research and Development	-$	32,702,351

Selling Expenses	-$	190,763,714
Administrative Expenses	-$	54,503,918
Other income	$	10,900,784
Other Expenses	-$	21,801,567
Taxes	-$	13,353,460
Net Income	$	24,799,283

STEP 1: Ask yourself What do I need to convey? **You need to convey the middle steps that took place to diminish the profits**

STEP 2: Select the table from A2 to B10

STEP 3: Go to "Insert" tab, select the Waterfall Icon

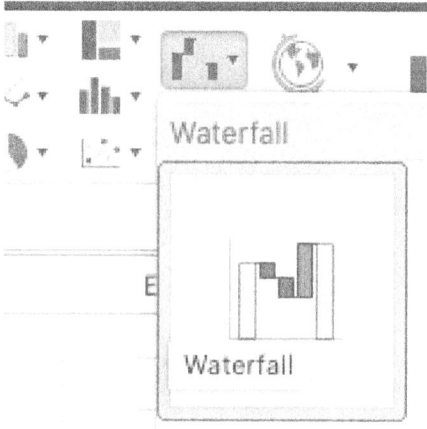

You will get this chart

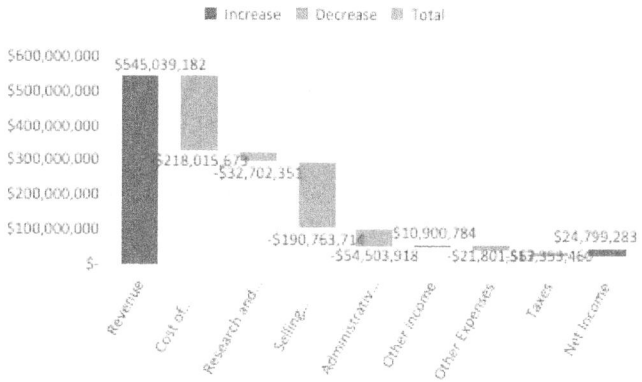

Notice how this Chart fill the INCREASE BARS with one color and the DECREASE BARS another color. Also notice how each bar starts where the previous bar ended, thus, creating a sequence of middle steps that leads to the end result.

So, the first bar is the Revenue (Increase), and then you can notice that the 2 biggest expenses are Cost of production and Selling Expenses. At first glance, those expenses are the primary reason for the little profits. So, the management team should take a look at that first. If nothing can be done there, then they may need to check Administrative expenses and figure out a way to spend less.

Although controlling expenses is important, the best approach is to try to increase revenue, but hey, some efficiency is always needed.

SITUATION:

Open file Chapter9ex2.xlsx

Now, you want to know how the equity of your company grew over the past 4 years. Here is the data.

START $ 8,283,762

YEAR 1	$	500,392
YEAR 2	-$	2,839,584
YEAR 3	$	4,928,161
YEAR 4	$	2,947,562

STEPS: Just repeat the steps from the previous exercise and you will get this chart.

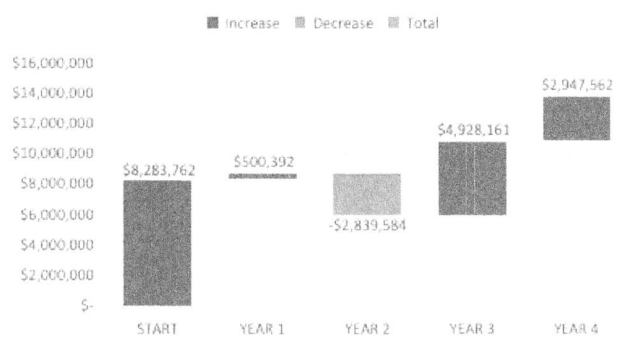

Notice how you started with 8 million, and lost some of it in year 2. But the company did something great in year 3 to recover from that lost and grew it equity substantially.

This is the power of a Waterfall chart, you get to see the middle steps, and can profit from the intel you get.

CONGRATULATIONS! This is how you use a Waterfall (Bridge) Charts.

MORE EXERCISES:

- Chapter9ex3.xlsx

QUICK CHAPTER SUMMARY:

- Waterfall Charts are useful to emphasize the middle steps that led to an end result.
- Are great also to show increases and decreases on a single variable over time.

CHAPTER 10

CHART TYPE #7
SCATTERPLOT CHARTS

We only have 2 types of charts left! So, let's continue.

Scatterplot Charts are not as used as all the previous charts that you have learned throughout this book, but they are quite useful in the field of statistics.

They use X and Y axis to show the distribution of values around 2 variables. Each value is represented in the "map" as a little dot. When you visualize lots of dots (lots of values) you can find patterns.

That said, the main use for Scatterplot Charts is to find whether certain given data has a pattern or not, and to show WHERE most of the values are found.

SITUATIONS TO USE SCATTERPLOT CHARTS:

- You face a situation where you have lots of values, 2 variables and you need to find a pattern or relationship:
  - Value of the car budget vs compared to household income
  - Sales compared to Time spent face to face with prospects
  - Total sales ticket compared to Net Worth of the client.
  - Etc

SITUATIONS TO AVOID USE SCATTERPLOT CHARTS:

- **You need to convey proportion of a whole.** You simply can't do it.
- **You need to compare the total value of several variables.** Not suitable for this task.

- You need to communicate and show development over time
- You need to show subcategories of a whole

SHOW TIME! (Open file Chapter10ex1.xlsx)

SITUATION:

Now you are the financial advisor for car retailer. You need to figure out whether the yearly income of a prospect influences the kind of car he buys or not. That way you can create an strategy to increase sales.

YEARLY INCOME OF THE CUSTOMER		PRICE OF THE CAR HE BOUGHT	
$	216,679	$	108,340
$	274,459	$	54,892
$	635,997	$	127,199
$	672,828	$	269,131

$	409,720	$	163,888
$	792,201	$	237,660
$	790,589	$	158,118

STEP 1: Ask yourself What do I need to convey? **You need to find the price tag of the car related to the yearly income of the customers**

STEP 2: Select the table from A2 to B89

STEP 3: Go to "Insert" tab, select the Scatter Icon

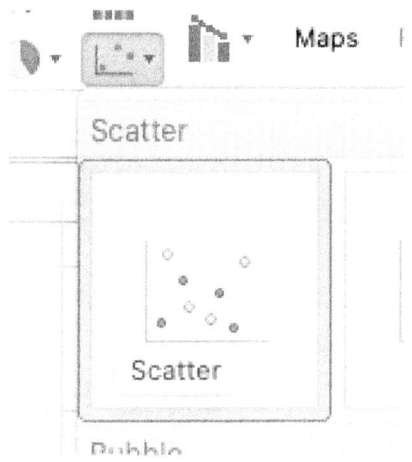

You will get the next chart

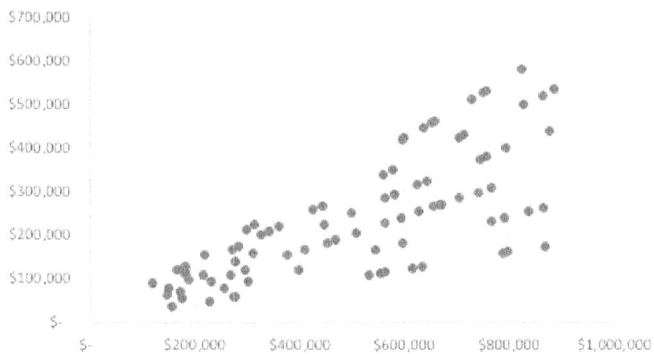

There are several things to notice in this chart:

- The X axis shows the yearly income of the customers that bought a car
- The Y axis shows the price tag of the car they bought
- Inside the cart you can find an interesting pattern. Although there are some customers that buy low-priced cars according to their incomes, there are others that rather buy more expensive cars with the same yearly income.
- Nevertheless, we can say with confidence that to a great extent, the. Yearly income of the customer does

determine the average amount he spends when buying a car.

SITUATION

Open file Chapter10ex2.xlsx

Try to find the relationship between supermarket spending and yearly income. Here is the data

YEARLY INCOME OF THE CUSTOMER	SUPERMARKET SPENDING
$ 39,630	$ 12,596
$ 96,534	$ 14,270
$ 58,370	$ 11,903
$ 32,187	$ 14,652
$ 76,559	$ 12,750
$ 68,818	$ 12,725
$ 62,573	$ 10,717
$ 90,692	$ 12,150

STEP 1: Ask yourself What do I need to convey?

STEP 2: Select the table

STEP 3: Go to "Insert" tab, select the Scatter Icon

In this situation, you will find that there is no relationship between yearly income and supermarket spending. The dots are all over the place.

CONGRATULATIONS! Scatterplot Charts are now in your toolkit. Let's move to the last type of chart.

QUICK CHAPTER SUMMARY:

- Scatter Charts are great to show the relationship between 2 variables
- Are great to find patterns that are important to decision making processes

CHAPTER 11

CHART TYPE #8
HISTOGRAM CHARTS

Histogram Charts are used specifically to show distribution of a specific variable. In other words, to convey how many times (frequency) you are getting the same variable amount.

Histogram charts are normally used in surveys and the X axis usually shows something like age of the people that answered the survey. You can also measure visitor time at a store, number of calls it takes to make a sale, etc.

As you may notice, Histogram Charts have a great application at finding unknown answers to a given question, and those answers could give you an edge at your current job.

SITUATIONS TO USE HISTOGRAM CHARTS:

- You face a situation where you need to convey the frequency and distribution that a certain variable repeats itself in order to find a pattern and become better:
  - How many times does a salesperson needs to call the prospect before he closes the sale?
  - How old are the people that is buying our product?
  - How many minutes does it takes to render this service?

SITUATIONS TO AVOID HISTOGRAM CHARTS:

- **You need to compare the total value of several variables.** Not suitable for this task.

- **You need to communicate and show development over time**
- **You need to show subcategories of a whole**
- **Everything else you learned throughout this book can't be done with an histogram chart**

SHOW TIME! (Open file Chapter11ex1.xlsx)

SITUATION:

You are getting a hard time as a sales manager and one of your ideas is to measure the amount of calls a salesperson needs to make to the same prospect in order to close the sale (from the 1st approach until the end of the sales process). Open the exercise file and find the complete table.

CLIENT	# OF CALLS
The Atom	7
X-Men	5
Asterix	9
Maximus	7
Conan the Barbarian	7
Ethan Hunt	7
Tsunade	6
Aquaman	3

STEP 1: Ask yourself What do I need to convey?

STEP 2: Select JUST THE B COLUMN OF THE TABLE (From B2 to B89)

STEP 3: Go to "Insert" tab, select the Histogram Icon

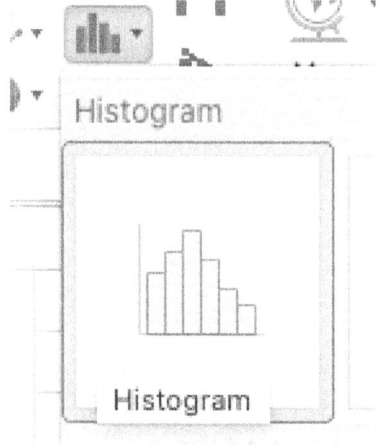

And you will probably get an strange Chart like this one

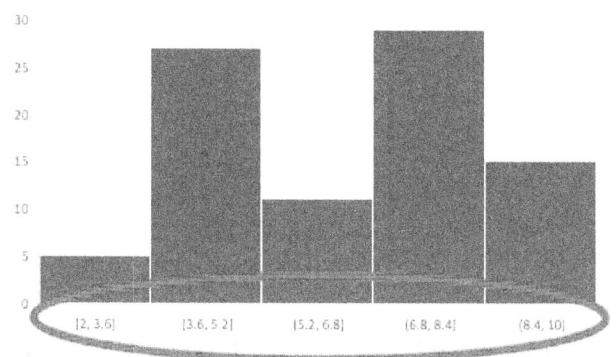

What is the problem with this chart? If you look closer to the X axis labels, they are showing results from 2 to 3.6, then from 3.6 to 5.2, etc. Thus, creating a histogram of 5

bins. But the results range from 2 to 10, and we want whole numbers (because you can't make 1 and a half sales call). Because of that. You need to show 8 bins instead of 5.

How can you solve that?

STEP 4: Double Click one of the bins (bars) and you will get a window called "**FORMAT DATA SERIES**" like this one.

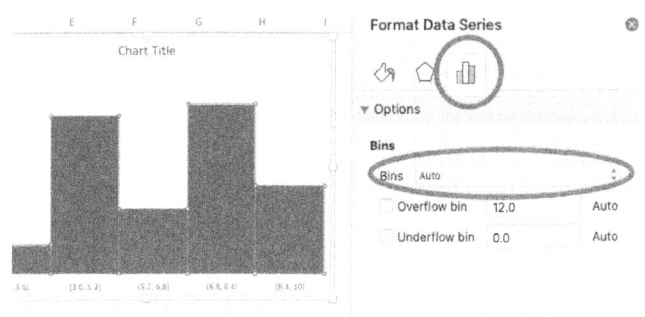

Notice how the Bins are in "Auto" Mode. You need to change that.

STEP 5: Click on Auto to deploy a panel of several options. In that panel you need to choose **BIN WIDHT**

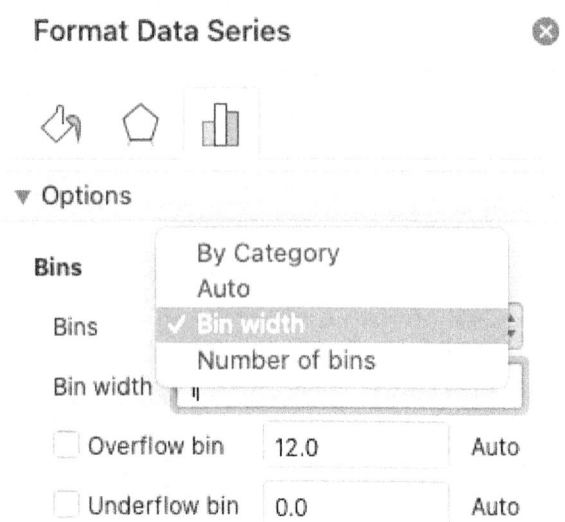

STEP 6: I want you to interpret BIN WIDHT as the "Variable **Range** that you want to show in each bin". Because we want 1 bin for each variable, please write 1 and press enter

Bins

Bins	Bin width	⌄

Bin width	1

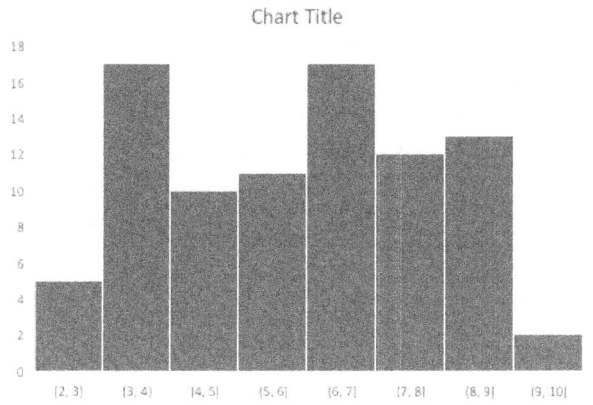

That's it! Now the first bin shows just 1 result per bin. Notice how the most repetitive number is 3 calls. With that insight, something could be implemented to train sales executives to try to get the sale in just 3 calls instead of 6, 7 or 8.

CONGRATULATIONS!! YOU COMPLETED ALL THE EXERCISES AND NOW OU CAN CALL YOURSELF AN EXCEL CHARTS NINJA!

GO OUT FOR SOMETHING TO EAT AND HAVE SOME FUN! YOU DESERVE IT

In the last chapter you'll get some extra advice on how to become an overall Excel Ninja!

QUICK CHAPTER SUMMARY:

- Histogram Charts are used to convey frequency and distribution
- Are not as used as the Bar, Pie and Line Charts, but are quite useful in some situations.

CHAPTER 12

QUICK FINAL TIPS

CONGRATULATIONS!! You finished the exercises and now you are an EXCEL CHARTS NINJA! It was a great journey.

This book wouldn't be complete without a series of final recommendations that can help you even more

Here (in this short chapter) I can't teach you everything I'm going to recommend because they are extensive topics that would not fit in a few pages, it is also information that I teach deeply in other Excel books.

However, I want to make the following recommendations you with the hope that you recognize the main tools that you must learn to be an EXCEL NINJA.

WHY DO YOU NEED TO LEARN MORE FUNCTIONS?

There are hundreds of functions that can help you to better perform your work, however you may not know them. Sometimes a new function that you learn can save you hours of weekly work in the office.

The important thing to remember about functions is that they tend to relate to each other and become stronger tools when combined or in the form of nested formulas.

I'll give you an example you already know: VLOOKUP. The VLOOKUP function is quite strong and useful on its own, but when you learned to use IF together with VLOOKUP, three things happened:

1) You learned a new function: VLOOKUP

2) You learned a new function: IF

3) You learned a new tool: IF + VLOOKUP

When you learn just two functions you actually have three tools in your toolbox. That is, your tools are not just the number of functions you master, but also include the combinations you can make between those functions.

So, the more functions you know, the more combinations you can make and the more chances you have to become an Excel Champion.

That is why I created Excel Formulas Ninja! The purpose of Formulas Ninja is to teach you the TOP Formulas in Excel in an Easy and Fast Way!

Get your copy of Excel Formulas Ninja here!

"A STRAIGHTFORWARD, EXERCISE-BASED AND FAST WAY TO LEARN EXCEL FUNCTIONS" - *Employee from a State Department of Education*

"The book was engaging and encouraging by providing many examples and exercises. I will eagerly study the other

books in the series."

WHY DO YOU NEED TO LEARN KEYBOARD PIVOT TABLES?

Pivot Tables are the go-to tools for advanced data analysis! Whenever you are immersed in a gigantic amount of data and you need to take decisions based on that data, Pivot Tables are the way to go!

You can summarize thousands of rows and columns (literally thousands) in just a few seconds. You also can shape your summary to every imaginable way, in order to get relevant insight about your data.

Base your decisions in facts, not opinions! Buy your Pivot Tables Champion copy here!

"THIS BOOK IS SO GREAT! NOW I CAN ANALYZE GIANT DATABASES WITHIN SECONDS!" - *Sales Coordinator of a Wholesale Company.*

WHY DO YOU NEED TO LEARN KEYBOARD SHORTCUTS?

First of all, I want to recommend that you learn Excel keyboard shortcuts. Keyboard shortcuts are the easiest and fastest way to increase your productivity in Excel. You can easily cut your work time in half.

The reality is that there are more than 100 keyboard shortcuts. My recommendation is that you learn the 10 or 20 main ones. Which are the main ones? The ones you use the most depending the kind of work you have to do in Excel.

Some of those that everybody should use are:

Ctrl + C to copy a cell (with format too)

Ctrl + V to paste the cell that you copied

Ctrl + X to cut the cell (instead of copying it, you remove it from its cell to paste it in another cell)

Ctrl + to insert a column or row (selecting the column or row previously)

Ctrl - to delete a column or row (selecting the column or row previously)

Surely with these shortcuts you can move a little faster. But there are more that are quite useful.

"I WAS ABLE TO SAVE COUNTLESS HOURS THANKS TO THIS BOOK!"- Department Store Manager

WHY DO YOU NEED TO LEARN CONDITIONAL FORMATTING?

You will agree that the human eye identifies faster the colors and shapes than numbers. For the same reason, traffic lights have colors instead of numbers or words.

The conditional formatting in Excel is used to add colors or shapes when certain conditions are met, making the data user-friendly and giving the opportunity to recognize patterns within the data.

Imagine for a moment that you have a table with 100 data and you need to find the values that are closest to the average.

Option 1: The first option is to use the AVERAGE function and then manually search for those values within the table.

Option 2: The fastest and easiest option is to use Conditional Format so that Excel automatically colors the data that is closest to the average, and that's it, you'll have the data you need highlighted in the color you want in a few seconds, it doesn't matter if your table has 100, 1000 or 10000 numbers.

If you would like to search for the 10 highest values within a table, you can do so. If you would like to focus only on data that is less than the average, you can color them automatically. If you want to identify the data that are between 2 values, you can do it in less than 30 seconds.

That is why I recommend conditional formatting. Becoming a Conditional

Formatting Champion will allow you to find the most relevant information.

Get your copy of Conditional Formatting Champion here!

"THIS GREAT AND EASY TO UNDERSTAND BOOK TEACHES A VERY USEFUL WAY TO ANALYZE DATA" - *Accounting Manager of a Sportswear Company*

WHY DO YOU NEED TO LEARN TO USE CHARTS AND DASHBOARDS?

Charts are, by excellence, the way to communicate quantitative information in the business world, in non-profit organizations, in schools, in governmental organizations, in health areas, in sports, etc.

It's very simple, if you want to effectively communicate your numerical data, you need to master the Excel Charts. That includes the use of tables and the correct positioning of them, the selection of the data that you need, the Chart Type selection and the modification of the parameters of the chart.

Additionally, it becomes necessary that you learn to discover what a chart wants to "tell you". Correctly analyzing the data in a chart usually leads to better decisions.

If you want to make better decisions in your job or company, it is very likely that becoming an Excel Charts and Graphs Champion will benefit you

I WOULD LOVE TO READ YOUR COMMENTS

Before you go, I would like to tell you Thank You for buying my book. It is my wish that the information you obtained in **EXCEL CHARTS & GRAPHS NINJA** helps you in your job or business, and that you can have greater productivity and more free time to use it in the activities that you like the most.

I realize that you could have chosen among several other Excel books but you chose **EXCEL CHARTS & GRAPHS NINJA** and you invested your time and effort. I am honored to have the opportunity to help you.

I'd like to ask you a small favor. <u>**Could you take a minute or two and leave a Review of EXCEL CHARTS & GRAPHS NINJA on Amazon?**</u>

This feedback will be very appreciated and will help me continue to write more courses that help you and a lot more people.

Share your comments with me and other readers

ABOUT THE AUTHOR

Henry E. Mejia is passionate about progress and goal achieving, he also loves to run and exercise. He works in the insurance industry and likes to invest in the stock market. While doing that, he devotes some time to create Excel written courses like this one, in order to help people to achieve their professional goals.

Henry also realized that the vast majority of people use a lot of their work time in front of the computer. That time could be used in more productive or more enjoyable activities, only if people knew how to use Excel a little better.

The goal of Henry's books is to open the door for workers and business owners to use Excel more efficiently, so they can have more and better growth opportunities, progress and free time.

Printed in Great Britain
by Amazon